Praise for Danita Geltner's
BEING A CITY GIRL, I SCREAMED

In "Being a City Girl, I Screamed" Geltner captures the cadence of caring. Her observations and imaginings whittle intimacy into a fine needle to the heart. Let there be salt, as she writes, and praise for ancestors and dirt, and also for Danita. The arrival of this vision and voice is cause to celebrate.
Laura Flanders, The Laura Flanders Show, @GRITlaura, @TheLFShow

Elegant, evocative, timeless poetry, prose, and narration for the modern age, in short form and in long, by a sensitive observer of the internal and external processes of our lives.
Dr. David Rind, NASA Emeritus, Columbia University

Read and re-read "Being a City Girl, I Screamed" and be transfixed by the kaleidoscopic insights Geltner shares. Startling, the order of her words, rupturing ordinary memory. Experience the danger and physicality of a dreamlike downhill ride on The Horse, or slip into her gaze as she stares through the eyes of The Garden Gnome. Reminding one of Antonio Porchia's Voices, Geltner's haikus embed meaning in an incalculable manner, one pops up then another and another...like a succession of holy koans, each one invites stillness, mystery and revelation.
Elizabeth Streb, Choreographer of STREB EXTREME ACTION; Director of STREB LABORATORY For ACTION MECHANICS (SLAM). Author of "How to Become an Extreme Action Hero".

This author has created a world full of feeling that has taken me on a journey deep inside myself. Amazing! Wonderful!

J. K. Lambert, Designer / Design Director, Random House, 1973-2003

Geltner's poetry has a natural lyricism without ever losing its potency. This is especially true of her haiku: delicious amuse-bouches that linger on the tongue and longer in the mind. Her sense of humor, vulnerability, and wiry wit seem to effortlessly flow in this substantive collection.

David Sisco, Author, "Mastering College Musical Theatre Auditions"
Composer, Voice Teacher & Coach
davidsisco.com

Danita Geltner's poems cut to the core of what it means to be human, slipping effortlessly between the internal world where thoughts and emotions reign, and the external world where beauty and fragility abound. She has modernized the haiku in a way few poets could, yielding insights that will stop you on the page. This book is like the best kind of friend— warm, surprising, and completely unafraid to ask The Big Questions. Geltner is a student of the city and the soul, and her poetry is packed with the wisdom and charm of someone who's learned them well.

Stephanie Paterik, Poet, Journalist, Managing editor of Adweek

BEING A CITY GIRL,
I SCREAMED

BEING A CITY GIRL, I SCREAMED

DANITA S GELTNER

City Girl Press
New York
2017

Cover photo: "Grey" by Danita Geltner
Back photo by Thomas Gentile
Author photo by David Rind

For Tommy G.
who goes to the ocean
to lose his mind
and find his soul

CONTENTS

PART 1 THOUGHTS   1
PART II WAITING TO GO ON   33
Leading Lady   35
A Force Carried Him   37
Fallen Feathers   39
Passage   41
Being a City Girl, I Screamed   43
What is Necessary?   45
Waiting to Go On   47
The Ride   49
On a Small Patch of Earth   51
The Garden Gnome   53
Between Me and My Poem,
    the Strawberry   55
Buried Treasure   57
The Horse   59
Someone's Missing   61
Ode to Salt   63
In the Land of Dreams   65
Self Portrait as Fragment   67
Sirens Sound in My Sleep   69
Excommunication   71
Home from Highway One   73
Not Today   75
In Lael Years   77
For Lynn Emanuel   79
The Woman   81
Hunger   83

It   85
To You and You and You   87
ACKNOWLEDGEMENTS   89
ABOUT THE AUTHOR   91

PART 1

THOUGHTS

1

I dreamed a Haiku
something about summertime
long days forgotten

2

A puzzle called self
a few pieces each day make
me laugh with surprise

3

Inside a room of
imagination D talks
with her mirror-self

4

Thoughts travel faster
than the Body arriving
ahead of clock-time

5

Reality and
dreams make wonderful lovers
but awkward parents

6

When disappointment
smashes the body, the heart
must reconfigure

7

A thought strikes me in
the head as if it has no
respect for its home

8

Castles in the sand
gone too soon, castles in the
mind build extensions

9

Childhood lingers in
the kitchen trying to re-
capture what was lost

10
Some ideas are
not meant to be understood
until late in life

11
Hold Beliefs loosely
for they need the chance to play
experiment, fail

12
Listen to the heart
beating in the night music
no one invented

13

Just before dawn the
heart recites a monologue
never before heard

14

Thoughts ask, "am I here
because of you or are you
here because of me?"

15

D wonders how well
her present self knows her past
and her future selves

16

My computer does
not care what shape my body
is in or my heart

17

Tick tock tick tock in
the night, tiny sound with a
powerful message

18

Lies argue with Truth
until Reality shifts
each one's perspective

19

I step out each day
as my own leading lady
amazed by the script

20

Fill in a blank day
with wild colors, and scribble
over the borders

21

The present moment
demands full attention just
like the last one did

22

Wizened King Tired yawns
"I am more than my people
know how to handle"

23

Millions of raindrops
will find their way home tonight
it's simple for them

24

Transparent layers
of thought blend future with past
rewriting today

25

Words in the highest
branches of my mind blossom
then fall to the ground

26

Life as theater
Ego meets Psyche each day
a drama unfolds

27

I would like to be
recognized for my genius
that's all I'm asking

28

The mind is a time
machine altering present
past and future thoughts

29

Once a decision
is made, rejected choices
lick their wounds and wait

30

It is the sequence
Dearest Author that renders
our words valuable

31

Childhood remains a
magical place on the near
side of a forest

32

Being loved as a
child stays stored in the body
to help with tough times

33

Did six year old me
know how important she would
be to me someday

34

Let's find the place where
Time goes, and when we do, we
might decide to stay

35

In the season called
Youth, First-Love ends, in order
to be remembered

36

"Childhood is so short,
why does it last so long?" asked
sister of brother

37

Beneath a hero's
monument, mistakes not at
rest agitate bones

38

D likes going back
to the beginning because
it is always there

39

"Airbrushing away
wrinkles," declares Time, "is an
act of violence"

40

My poems woke me
in the night like restless kids
wanting to be heard

41

The living and the
dead mix freely in my dreams
all of us equal

42

Vacation spills out
from a suitcase disturbing
all that used to be

43

Bossy King Busy
thinks if he stays busy he
shall always stay King

44

A diary-self
in her teens invites D to
remember the past

45

Sugar, butter and
flour play in the kitchen
like three childhood friends

46

Fold an idea
into imagination
knead gently, then wait

47

A tiny angel
wing flutters in from sleep just
like a real image

48

Poems are never
finished, as they float away
they look back and wink

49

Eternity waits
forever for me to come
to believe she's here

50

I speak poetry
an Ancient Language first shared
telepathically

51

Love stayed after the
Church broke her heart because she
promised Faith she would

52
Love took dogma by
the hand saying, "I'll stay with
you till you grow up"

53
Technology feeds
off humans then runs on no
food, water or sleep

54
When I have nothing
left to do I shall dust the
inside of cabinets

55
The body has a
mind of its own with free will
and no will at all

56
I tuck part of me
in bed, another part of
me stays up writing

57
The performance of
Life calls for attention to
detail and applause

58

When toast bursts into
flame, hunger leaves the body
for more urgent things

59

The movie ended
before D was ready to
face the world again

60

Life presents itself
anew each day such that no
one can master it

61
Practice patience with
life, treat it like a young child
give kindness and love

62
To wake up feeling
HAPPY TO BE ALIVE is
a gift of great size

63
Reality and
Truth don't always dialog
calmly together

64

Writing my life like
a book with cliff-hangers and
a surprise ending

65

When success came my
friend said, "now I am happy
but I am not free"

66

Hubris crushes man
like a foot steps on a bug
Unexpectedly

67

An empty chair at
the dinner table told the
children everything

68

Pain is a single
timeless note unifying
all people on earth

69

Paranoia speaks
like it knows The Truth, but it's
goal is fear, not truth

70

Communication
stops when stubborn 'old beliefs'
create a roadblock

71

Dormant thoughts wake up
startled, after many years
of hibernation

72

"MeMeMe," either
a high pitched note or— our
Primal human cry

73

Lies wrestle Truth till
Reality referees
and both cry uncle

74

Sleep interrupted
the physical quandary
of being human

75

Everyone sees through
their own beliefs their own world
knowing no other

76
'Interpretation'
is the best anyone can
do with what they hear

77
When scared, D's poems
hide inside a drawer and speak
to no one at all

78
When the heart breaks the
Mind asks the Body to share
the experience

79

Emotions create
a dust storm hiding the real
story far below

80

When life's rough edges
cut deeply, the heart bleeds, no
band aid can stop it

81

The hardest thing to
remember is that not all
people think like me

82

Timeless moments end
abruptly in a cascade
of forgotten tasks

83

In blackness a thin
line of light coming from a
closed door is enough

84

Emotion: the
force that drives thoughts into
Physical reality

85
Dreaming up poems
in a high-rise while workmen
fix the street below

86
Everything that has
the word MY in front of it
is terrifying

87
Memories replay
an original moment
with added feelings

88

Surgeons find matter
inside the brain, not thoughts, not
ideas, not dreams

89

One day I will shed
my spacesuit in order to
go on exploring

90

My last thought shall be
special not knowing with whom
how, where or when

PART II

WAITING TO GO ON

LEADING LADY

I leave my house pretending
I'm an actress
No— more than an actress—

a glamorous leading lady in my own film
Costumes conjure character
One day, cast as a spy,
with an Audrey-Hepburn-in-Budapest style,
dramatic brim pulled low over one eye

I sleuth between closing subway doors
"Take my seat," a gentleman stands up for me

I cast him in the next scene

A FORCE CARRIED HIM

When he met her he thought he knew himself

He grew up in Queens,
had a speech impediment,
didn't learn to talk until he was six

The first day of school his teacher sent him home with a note,
"Your child is being ridiculed, no one can understand him."

Many times he escaped through his bedroom window
Once he returned to find
all access locked
He dodged fists and belts and pointing fingers
His father threatened,
"I hope you grow up to have a son just like you,"
shaking his fist at the boy
who knew he'd never have children
Never

At seventeen
he dropped out of school
went to Vietnam
stayed two tours
"Before each mission we'd pick up our ammo, we'd pick up our
drugs.
What did it matter, our life expectancy was one and a half missions."
He survived thirty-three and a half missions

When he got home
he wasn't met by crowds with praise

He threw away his uniform
became a body builder
a black belt

A force carried him
from Oakland to Queens

No one knew at night
he screamed
dodged bullets
hid under his bed when noises
grew too loud

She met him in a club
caught by the gaze of his pale blue eyes
he had a good wink

She believed
he could change
over time
with love
but
every time he saw red
he began the same rant
"damn traffic lights!"

First low
almost sane
By the time she opened the car door
waiting for the light to turn green
she wasn't leaving a man
she was leaving a force field
capable of killing

FALLEN FEATHERS

A small yellow body
Slips from the ecosystem
Leaving a broken circle

Six-foot wings
Shadow an oil-slicked sea
Searching for fish

Poison rains from planes
Over cornfields, while sparrows
Softly chirp nearby

An apparition in a Carolina Green
Parrot hat refuses to leave
Her old plantation

Like a tree full of mockingbirds at dusk
Politicians repeat phrases
To the wind

Pigeons and gulls
Find fast food garbage
Undisturbing

When an instinctual alarm
Malfunctions, Martins arrive
Too late to eat

Far from the life they knew
Dodo Birds thrive
On canvases in museums

The Stork's existence is secured
Only by bringing babies to earth
From heaven

A poet imagines
King Vulture
Eating the world

Swans break up the floating
Moon that crowds
Their vanishing pond

Plastic flamingos greet guests
Who pause to make sure
They're not real

PASSAGE

Here is me walking a deserted beach in the name of the father
looking for ghosts

Here is me dragging my ten foot shadow
pleased to not leave me alone

Here is me finding a shard of sea glass
placing it in a bowl waiting for sunrise

Here is me standing still on the old wooden pier looking down
at the desecration of worms

And here I am
screaming into the wind something about betrayal

Begging for The Sanity and The Reason
and The Heart as if they were

The Holy Trinity
Here I am

In another world remembering
the smudge of ash, the slithering snake

The apostle's kiss— would you still leave me
alone on this lush green planet hurling itself through space?

Here I am
striving to get through to you

Reaching down from
the top of my own consecrated mountain

Holding out forever and ever
in my arms

BEING A CITY GIRL, I SCREAMED

Knowing nothing about low tide,
crabs and what all-sorts-of-fishy-things do
in one-foot-deep water

At first I thought it was disturbed,
coming after me,
seaweed tangled blur
far from shore
stranger that I am

I bent down to watch more closely,
as the rippled surface stilled
What's this?

He's not alone,
claws of another crab beneath him
"He's fucking," I said,
"he's not disturbed
he's not coming after me
he's fucking."

Shift of light
No— he's not fucking
He's protecting a baby
He's a mother crab protecting his baby
Clouds part—

"In Vietnam," my ex-husband said,
"we could not tell, *we could not tell*,
were they mothers cradling babies
or bombs?"

WHAT IS NECESSARY?

To sit in an Adirondack chair
on a bluff
high above the tide
while the mind
constructs a boat?

To construct a boat
smell mahogany wood
anticipate the craft
hands kept busy?

To drift in a boat
already constructed
no leaks
a rhythmic motion
360 degrees of possibility?

To travel in that boat
across a school of light
jumping silver
diving wings
the smell of salt air—

What is necessary?
To have an experience?
Or... to imagine one?

WAITING TO GO ON

My mind wanders to the creek
in the yard where I grew up
beside a willow tree with its branches close together

We called it our space ship
It had a captain's station and a control room
My Burmese cat is with me in the tree
She climbs fast
like a lizard
soon she's higher than the house

Even though my mind wanders
I hear every word on stage,
"It must be the medication."
Clare has just spoken
Bob nods

Clare, Bob, and I met in summer stock the year
Katz introduced The Wandering Mind Technique
"Pull up an image in your mind
that helps with the scene and channels anxiety."
No one questioned Katz, he was brilliant

Mom told me not to be an actress
a thought that never leaves my mind
I leap over it every time
I go on stage

Bob begins his monologue
Clare is trembling
soon I'll smash the glass I'm holding
and begin to scream
"A combination of sweetness and fire,"
the director said of my character

Clare and Bob are fighting now
his hands around her neck
I tighten my grip on the glass
I close my eyes
I see the cat leap from branch to branch

I don't remember screaming
when the branch broke

"Damn games children play
get down from that tree!"
My mother in her shirtwaist dress,
"What's wrong with you girl, your mind's a million miles away."
She had a tiny waist and fire in her eyes

The audience has no idea
what will happen next

THE RIDE

Sixteen hands high, obsidian eyes,
a snort like the devil himself.

I rode him bareback
down a steep hill
when the moon was full
and the river swelled high.

Uncontainable current
slammed riverbank walls.

"What a kind horse,"
I spoke softly to him,
my body swaying back and forth,
squeezing with my thighs to keep from falling.
Mossy-wet rocks, steady hoofs,
"slooooow, eeeeeeasy,"
I egged him on to the exact spot I wanted,
leaned into his side, grabbed a fist full of mane,
slid,
then dropped to the ground.

He stood still, I stepped back
when, for an instant, our eyes met in another world,
another time.

The sinews of his flesh rippled, rose,
and the coarse black hair
across his back
bristled with silvery light.
Then, with the power of a god,
he took off.

My legs trembled,
I lost strength.
Two soldiers approached
took each of my arms.
"Where is he?"
They gave a shake,

"where is he?"
And the wind whispered back
Gone.

ON A SMALL PATCH OF EARTH

The thought, *terror is unavoidable*
coincided with a sudden squawk
a bird across the lake

Quivering from the last shot fired
I'm lost formed a precept,
an anti-home in her mind

She envied every moment but the present
How fresh the spider's web
How still the early morning air

Somewhere, not here, a rooster crowed
Somewhere, not here, an ocean found land
Somewhere, not here, a plane banked in the sky

The decision to head back
became concrete
She set the gun down

There will be an inquiry
they will demand a written report
time, place, reason

THE GARDEN GNOME

Traveling through earth as a fish swims through water, Gnome was more than a stake in the ground. Admiring the Romantics, fairy tales and Proust, Gnome's head held more than anyone could imagine. As fallen leaves carpeted the earth, Gnome took pride in his home. Eight-foot shadows followed his holy days. He feared his dark side. At night, he walked to the Land of Light to be fed for his life back home. Last fall a bright red mum stopped him in his stride, suggesting holiday clothing. In summer he remembered snow-sculptures falling from the sky. "Hoarfrost forgive me, for intruding upon your beauty," another gnome once heard him say. Gnome knew his last thought would be special, because it would be his last. When the time came, a speckled finch landed on his shoulder, cocked her tiny head. Gnome thought about a rush of blood to a wound in the dark, without sound. Gnome's broken arm remains in the junk drawer in the kitchen. His body was lost long ago.

BETWEEN ME AND MY POEM, THE STRAWBERRY

My poem refuses to talk about my father's death, but I don't refuse. I want to talk about the last bite I saw my father take.

My poem says. "No, don't do it. Put it in code. Use metaphor."

"No. I won't. This is about something real. I was there. I was with him. He wanted to die. He had quit eating. But I wanted to keep him alive, so I brought him his favorite food, strawberries."

"Stop." says my poem.

"I won't. I can't. He'd been refusing to eat for days, many days."

"Stop."

"I can't. Please understand. Dad had Alzheimer's. Mother had just died. It was incredibly sad."

"Stop, don't say it was incredibly sad. Let the reader feel how you felt as you offered your dad a strawberry, how you both felt after your Mother died."

"I can't."

"Why not?"

"Because now it's become too real."

Now, I just need to be alone, with the blue sky and the knowing way the sun shown that day across my father's face. The delicate way he looked at me.

The way he spoke without words.

Don't ask me to eat any more.

BURIED TREASURE

Here is a woman, see her 5' 2" body standing behind a glass door. Waving. Call her mother. Feel the energy she radiates through her body, out the door, along the sidewalk, leading up to a curved driveway, an automatic garage door.

Here comes a man and a girl pulling up in a car. Call this, "coming home." Call the man father. Call the girl, daughter.

Here comes a dog who cannot run fast enough to greet them. Father, mother, daughter, dog, the cables of a bridge, the roots of a Giant Sequoia.

Create a structure for them to live. Make it brick. Fill it with a golden thread from a shag carpet, a frozen pea hiding beneath a kitchen chair, a portrait of grandfather, disturbed from dusting, hanging crooked on the wall.

Stop.

Wrap everything up in swaddling cloth. Lay it all inside a manger. Add The Magi bearing gifts: a lost tooth, a braid of hair, a chip of china. Consider worship. Forget not the power of Ancient Ancestors buried deep within the earth.

THE HORSE

Let the wind echo back from The Cave of Yesterday.
Hear these words resound off its ancient wise walls,

He's not here.

When soldiers arrive, intent on finding him,
let me explain.

He was like an over-worshipped god who got spoiled.
He had to be taken back into Heaven to be recycled,
I tell you, he's gone.
Let the soldiers take me away.

Do not try to follow.
That was yesterday when the horse was mine.
Black as a widow's dress,
a snort like the devil himself.
No one could tame him, everyone tried.

I rode him bareback down a steep hill.
A thousand puzzle pieces falling from the sky.
No dogs, no cats, just a cloud of angels singing
The Hallelujah Chorus, sonic voices, surround sound.

We rode steadily down.
The hill alive with displeasure, *you're hurting me.*

At the bottom an uncontainable force slammed the riverbank wall.
We rode atop its slippery crest. Delirious current sprayed our bod-
ies, my tattooed flesh, his fantasy fur. We stopped.

I wanted a sign. Then heard, *Fire!*
Fire! On the bridge that separates reality from fantasy.

Go back to the scene in the wings.
See the cast of characters eager to be assigned their part,
a horse, black as a starless night,
a tattooed woman, naked as Eve in the garden,
a holy man, invisible, proud.
Call him imagination, give him a plot of his own, then take him
away.

Leave the plot, the woman, the horse. Set the whole scene on fire.
When soldiers arrive— let me explain.

SOMEONE'S MISSING

Fitting I'm not in the snapshot
with the three of them broadly smiling.
Can I forgive them—
Dad, in his favorite tennis sweater,
as if he just stepped off the court,
Mom in her paisley-print blouse,
Brother Pete wearing preppy glasses.

Forty years later
Pete hands that snapshot to me

    "Why aren't I in the picture?
    Wait a minute, maybe I'm the one
    taking it, you're all smiling at me."

    "No we're not,
    Mary took that picture."

    "Mary, my sister-in-law Mary?"

Pete turns the snapshot over,
hands it back to me.
I see. "Lunch at the Club, 1973"

1973. Of course.
That was the year I was in the hospital,
having cut my wrist,
the wrist attached to the arm
attached to the body

that weighed 80 pounds,
because it refused to eat,
because it couldn't find its place in the family,
because all the roles were taken
except for the role of fucked-up little sister,

I remember now.
I hand the picture back to my brother.

"Thanks for reminding me
how happy everyone was that year."

ODE TO SALT

Praise the salt in my kitchen with her own wooden bowl
sitting high on a shelf— Kitchen Royalty— with full authority

Praise the mighty saltiness of salt,
her ability to take charge,
her ability to change potatoes and carrots and lamb

Praise the ocean from whence she came
Praise the cliffs that hold her
Praise the sun for beaming separation: Let there be water

Let there be salt
Praise the shaker who keeps her together
Praise the hands who shake the shaker
Shaking salt free to be
Salt of the earth, salt of the sea

As in the sea, so in the blood
Praise the salt that courses through
My beating heart

Heart to heart
Praise the salt that seeps from my lover's skin
Praise the tongue that finds it

IN THE LAND OF DREAMS

I rule myself
as if I am three separate beings.

I give myself names: Danella,
Bichette, Tumah.

I give us no restrictions
such as scale or time,
gravity or space.

I command us, in the Land of Dreams, "Make use
of Danella's Tool Box full of multi-dimensional objects:
long-horned hammers, twelve-headed pliers."

In Bichette's Studio, I instruct us on how to use
whisper brushes, lacy colors,
and jelly-brain clay.

We frequent Tumah's Kitchen
in order to taste herbs Tumah herself invents
out of our past mistakes.

When I struggle I hear, "Call upon the wind."

When I am perplexed, Bichette suggests birds,
chiffon, bridges.

Danella teaches The Language of Light-Beam-Sound
which we practice, over and over without complaint,
until clarity resonates.

Tumah pulls, fresh from The Sea of Creation,
herb encrusted waves saying. "Do not be afraid to ride them."

In moments of great jubilee, we teach each other
how to travel faster than light so as not to be seen
by those who are not yet ready to see us.

SELF PORTRAIT AS FRAGMENT

D steps out of the magical land of childhood into the land of grown-ups with a Peace Sign dangling round her neck. D marches to stop a war: one foot in tradition while the other foot keeps the beat of her generation's music and drugs. D flies to Paris hoping to get away from 'Why Questions' that surround her every move like barbed wire. D falls head over heels into a prodigious ocean, fly-fish leaping, an infinite number of shapes. D hears, "Put this puzzle together without knowing the image." D hears, "Put this puzzle together until the image is your own."

SIRENS SOUND IN MY SLEEP

Too many hours at work leave bodies
passing thru me like vapor

I try not to attach to the person
man, woman, child

Perform your duties, senior nurse says

I pick up the scissors, quickly
I begin cutting their clothes
We're not here to save clothing

And yet

It was her clothing that woke me

Armani leggings, Dior platform heels,
the tiny black strap I cut from around her ankle

I hardly heard when the doctor said

"You can stop now"

EXCOMMUNICATION

The Bishop arrived late
　　as Bishops often do

It takes forty years, seven months and seven days
　　to become a Bishop

"One lump or two?" She turned to the Bishop hoping
　　to serve him better

Have you ever seen a naked Bishop?

The truth is, a Bishop cannot be naked
　　or truth might be revealed

Before I was born, I understood the word Bishop to have
　　hidden meaning

Last night I surprised myself by finding a lost Bishop
　　(no one ever knew Bishops could be lost)

Bishops in exile, alone and afraid, off guard and broken
　　glow in the dark

Bishops in turmoil breath fire

It takes a Bishop to know a Bishop, that's why
　　there must always be two (thus the first syllable— bi)

If you decide to shop for a Bishop bring lots of money
    Bishops are expensive

And you must have already heard, Bishops never bargain
    and never go on sale

HOME FROM HIGHWAY ONE

What I remember now
is the half eaten lasagna
inside a white Styrofoam container

We left it inside the refrigerator
of the B & B where we stayed
on the coast of Northern California

In my mind, it's dark
inside the refrigerator
The lasagna is alone
The people who laughed,
drank wine, commented
    how good it is,
those people have gone

Three thousand miles away
in the middle of the night
I feel the horrible dark
cold of the refrigerator

No one talks about the aftermath
of the carefree days

We took the lasagna back
to the B & B because
we had to take something

or we'd be left
with a sudden chill
an extinguished candle flame

and the sound of metal chairs
scraping the hard rock floor

NOT TODAY

One day I shall write about the morning mother died. One day I shall be able to tell how quietly we sat together. How I gently took the sheet, covered her slightly open mouth, because I knew she'd want me to. How I closed her soft hazel eyes since she couldn't do it for herself. How I held her hand, stroking her fingers while the blood receded. How that morning unfolded like a well-written book, the last chapter needing to be reread again and again. There will come the day when I will be able to write about the phone call I made to the one person I thought would understand, help me get up, walk away. One day I will write about all these things, one day, but not today.

IN LAEL YEARS

In the future
everything will be measured in *Lael Years*...
From the moment I hit the water—
that will mark the end of time—
the beginning of the expression
in *Lael Years*...

Will I be conscious when I hit the water?
Am I conscious now?
Have you ever
looked over the side
of the George Washington Bridge?
It takes your breath away

I take off my jacket, my shoes, my purse
I leave them behind
as I walk from Manhattan to New Jersey
I turn back around, I continue walking
cars whiz by, a backdrop of white noise
perhaps I'm invisible

As my body falls, *Lael Years* will pass by quickly
What kind of splash will I make? Feet first?
I would be so small, like an arrow or a bullet
piercing the water

Time and space collide into critical mass
inside my head, I cover my ears, in this moment
I have no idea what anything means

The wind is more powerful than I imagined
I close my eyes
I envision leaning
opening my arms wide, like wings
I'll let the wind carry me down

I'll land like falling in snow, the imprint of an angel

"In *Lael Years*..."
That's how everything in the future, in my family
will be measured

Mom was two times *Lael Years* plus seven
Dad never grew out of his *Lael Years*
My brother will pass quickly through *Lael Years* and grow strong
I'm sorry, Mom
forever haunted by *Lael Years*— Twenty four
That's enough

FOR LYNN EMANUEL

I carry your poems with me, a sheath of second skin

Turn off the moon. I want—
a dark night alone with my feelings
'til your words become sound
A howl   A curse

I want—
that hungry dog
on the page where I screamed
to leap into my lilywhite bedlam

Tell me more

I want— a steamy closet
filled with holy things, I slip
easily into despair
Feed me cocktails
Pour me a too-tight-dress
Make it pulse
to match my mind

I want— to mingle with women,
share mirrors, clutch bags
Our sanity neatly folded
like mother's "take this sweetie"
twenty dollar bill

Yesterday it rained
like God was sweating the Apocalypse
I felt no compassion

When the dyke broke, I tore at my skin
then laughed when I should have cried

The rain beats harder now
Stand still and stick out your tongue
if you want to know the flavor of storm

This is our shadow-less night

Like a mongrel escaping shelter
I stand dripping beneath your window
Begging

I want more
Tell me more

THE WOMAN

Let the wind speak its truth from The Cave of Yesterday
Hear the words become an anthem that no one forgets,

He's not here, he's not here.

When soldiers arrive, intent on finding him,
I try to explain—

He was like a super hero that got spoiled.
So he went back to the stars to be reconstructed,
He's gone, I tell you. He's gone.
Don't argue.
Let the soldiers take me away.

That was yesterday, when a thousand puzzle pieces
tore loose from the sky.
The Hallelujah Chorus rained down like cats and dogs
as the horse and I picked our way slowly
to the bottom of a craggy old hill.
Rocks jumping out of our way.
The hill alive with displeasure.

At the bottom of the hill a river ran wild.
We rode atop its painted crest.
Uncontrollable current sprayed our bodies and clothes, my hand-
painted silk,
his fantasy fur.
Befuddled, we stopped.

Stood still.
Waited for a sign. Then heard, *Fire! Fire!*
On the bridge that reconstructs Fact with Fiction.

Go back.
Go back to the scene in the wings before the action begins.
See the cast of characters waiting to be discovered:
the horse nuzzles a piece of black fur.
the woman, searches for hand painted silk.
the man, holy and proud,
wanting a plot of his own— give it to him. Then take him away.

Let the woman and the horse be everything.

HUNGER

Remember the feral years when you looked at everyone
as food. Filling your plate with a piece of steak, salt,
pepper and blood.

Remember the cold days of February,
ravenous for hot, savory stews, thick gravy,
your need to be full.

Led by sensation,
you climbed six flights of stairs
then starved yourself numb in a one room flat
in Paris. The smell of the street drugged you to sleep
the aroma of freshly baked bread.

During the day you ate a carrot, a cup of broth,
a hard-boiled egg.

Late nights of passion
dark velvet cake
trembling, you court it
up to your lips
eyes close, still—
you deny.

Remember where and what you were
when they found you
a sliver on the street.

They took you away.
They made you wake up.
Then Elsa attacked you with a knife.
Ice cream slid to the floor.

IT

It strode violently across the stage,
listening to no one, cumbersome,
awkward

It lapped at the floorboards under the house
It screamed through the windows,
poked holes,
made tiny cracks

It rode horses, jumped fences, positioned
Itself with authority
It always kept the mystery alive
It shed its skin every seventh year

It flew thirty-seven thousand feet in the air,
did handstands on the wings of the plane,
blew kisses from the door
It danced with the clouds, teasing, "I'm hardly here."

It felt
everyone's pain
Once It reassured a pilot
when his hands began to shake

It hated re-entry
It carried a burden,
even as It winked in a crowd

It learned to respect the familiar, even as
It learned to sip quietly on the unknown

It made me feel beautiful
Twice It polished my toes

It learned when to be still and, after many years,
It learned how
not to frighten a child

It understood, not everyone
was meant to hear, to see,
to fly

To YOU and YOU and YOU

My sailboat is built with grace
and beauty, placed on the water
as if ready to sail, but
where is the wind?

My row boat is made, a perfect
hollowed out shell, the finest wood
found, cut with precision, but
where are the oars?

My yacht has been crafted over
time, without fail, instruments
sharpened, chrome polished, but
where is the fuel?

You are the fuel, the oars, the wind

ACKNOWLEDGEMENTS

I'd like to thank the editors of U.S. 1 Worksheets for publishing Being a City Girl, I Screamed; What is Necessary?; On a Small Patch of Earth (when it was titled She), and The Horse in earlier versions. I'd like to thank the publishers of the Edison Literary Review for publishing Hunger when it was titled Addiction. I'd like to thank the publishers of Podium, the literary magazine of the 92Y for publishing In the Land of Dreams. I'd like to thank the publishers of Pens On Fire for publishing It and Excommunication when Excommunication was titled Did You Know.

Thanks also to the publishers of U.S. 1 Worksheets Volume 56 for nominating the poem Being a City Girl, I Screamed for a Pushcart Prize in 2011.

I'd especially like to thank two wonderful poets who are also generous poetry teachers whom I have had the enormous pleasure of working with over the years: Jeanne Marie Beaumont and Erica Wright — thank you for sharing your treasures. Also, I'd like to give a personal hug of gratitude to several poetry buddies who have contributed timeless poetry moments to my poems, the joy of writing, and the necessity of sharing: Stephanie Paterik, Caroline Hagood, Patrick James — thank you for your poetic souls. And to Arlene Raven, writer mentor no longer here, nonetheless her voice is heard. And to composer David Sisco — we share in this journey. And to Jimmy Lambert, Laura Grooms, Elizabeth Streb and David Rind — every life I've ever lived, you've been there — this one, full of creative bursts, strikes me as especially grand... And to

Thomas Gentile — beyond words, I thank you. Last but not least, with humility and courage, I praise Creativity herself, in the end, she has her way through All People on Earth — may Love be the force. Amen

IN LAEL YEARS is written in honor of Lael Summer and to everyone, especially young people, who struggle with the disease of depression.

ABOUT THE AUTHOR

Danita Geltner's poetry has been nominated for a Pushcart Prize and published in U.S. 1 Worksheets, The Edison Literary Review, Podium, The Literary Journal of the 92 Street Y and Pens On Fire. Geltner has presented poems at Manhattan's Kiva Café, Brooklyn's Arcadia Studio and Princeton University. In October of 2012 Geltner began writing one or more haiku a day as a Facebook Project. To date She's written 2200 haiku with over 900 of them posted on Facebook, many accompanied with an original photograph. On November 14, 2014, six of her poems were put to music by composer David Sisco and sung by soprano Marie Mascari at Carnegie Hall.

Danita Geltner was born in Atlanta, Georgia and grew up in a rural area outside of Pittsburgh, Pennsylvania. She received a B.F.A. from the University of Pittsburgh, a Certificate Francaise from The Sorbonne, Paris, France, and an M.F.A. from The Maryland Institute, College of Art. Geltner has studied poetry with Jeanne Marie Beaumont, David Yezzi and Glen Maxwell at the 92 Street Y; Erica Wright at New York University; Marie Howe and Marie Ponsot at the Fine Arts Work Center in Provincetown, Massachusetts; and Afaa Michael Weaver at the renown Frost Place Poetry Workshop in New Hampshire.

In addition to poetry, Geltner taught Drawing, Color and Design at Rutgers University. Geltner's artwork, large-scale constructions, sculptures and two-dimensional were exhibited at P.P.O.W., ArtMart, and Grace Borgenicht Gallery in New York City. Geltner studied acting at HB Studios with John

Monteith and with Anna Deavere Smith/ADS workshop in San Francisco. Geltner studied voice with David Sisco of New York City and Mediation with the New York Peace Institute. Geltner has lived in New York City, since 1977, where she has had occasion to scream.

danitageltner.com

geltnerdanita@gmail.com